TIMELINE HISTORY

HOMES

From Caves to Eco-Pods

Elizabeth Raum

Heinemann Library
Chicago, Illinois

www.heinemannraintree.com
Visit our website to find out
more information about
Heinemann-Raintree books.

To order:
☎ Phone 888-454-2279
🖥 Visit www.heinemannraintree.com
to browse our catalog and order online.

Edited by Louise Galpine and Diyan Leake
Designed by Richard Parker
Original illustrations © Capstone Global Library Ltd 2011
Illustrated by Jeff Edwards
Picture research by Hannah Taylor

Originated by Dot Gradations Ltd
Printed and bound in China by CTPS

14 13 12 11 10
10 9 8 7 6 5 4 3 2 1

Library of Congress Cataloging-in-Publication Data
Raum, Elizabeth.
    Homes : from caves to eco-pods / Elizabeth Raum.
        p. cm. -- (Timeline history)
    Includes bibliographical references and index.
    ISBN 978-1-4329-3802-4 (hc) -- ISBN 978-1-4329-3810-9
(pb) 1. Dwellings--History. I. Title.
    GT170.R38 2011
    643'.109--dc22
                                    2009048949

Acknowledgments
The author and publisher are grateful to the following for
permission to reproduce copyright material: Alamy Images
pp. **7** top (© RIA Novosti), **10** top (© Arcticphoto), **12** bottom
(© Peter Horree), **16** (© Anna Stowe), **24** bottom (© View
Pictures Ltd); Corbis pp. **5** (Atlantide Phototravel), **6** (The
Gallery Collection), **11** bottom (Destination), **15** top (Nik
Wheeler), **17** top (Edward S. Curtis), **20**, **21** bottom (Reuters/
Thomas Mukoya), **22** (Bettmann), **24** top (Bettmann), **25** (The
Cover Story/Floris Leeuwenberg), **26** bottom (Art on File),
27 (Arcaid/Larraine Worpole); Getty Images pp. **7** bottom
(Riser/Andreas Stirnberg), **12** top (Dea Picture Library),
21 top (Popperfoto), **23** top (Iconica/Superstudio); Mary Evans
Picture Library p. **18**; Photolibrary pp. **4** (Wes Walker), **8** (Dan
Gair Photographic), **9** top (Jim Steinberg), **10** bottom (Michele
Falzone), **11** top (Egmont Strigl), **13** top (P. Narayan), **14**
(National Trust Photo Library), **15** bottom (Steve Vidler), **17**
bottom (M.A. Otsoa de Alda), **19** top (Walter Bibikow),
19 bottom (Raymond Forbes), **23** bottom (Doco Dalfiano);
Rex Features pp. **9** bottom (The Travel Library), **26** top
(Yan Morvan).

Cover photograph of shipping containers being used as
building material for apartments, reproduced with permission
of Corbis (Benedict Luxmore).

We would like to thank Ryan Hines for his invaluable help in
the preparation of this book.

Every effort has been made to contact copyright holders
of material reproduced in this book. Any omissions
will be rectified in subsequent printings if notice is given
to the publisher.

Contents

Historical time is divided into two major periods. BCE is short for "Before the Common Era"—that is, the time before the Christian religion began. This is the time up to the year 1 BCE. CE is short for "Common Era." This means the time from the year 1 BCE to the present. For example, when a date is given as 1000 CE, it is 1,000 years after the year 1 BCE. The abbreviation *c.* stands for *circa*, which is Latin for "around."

Any words appearing in the text in bold, **like this**, are explained in the glossary.

Homes for Everyone

Houses give us shelter from the weather and protect us while we sleep. In warm climates, houses provide shade. In colder climates, doors, windows, and thick walls protect us from freezing. Throughout history, poor people have built simple homes using materials such as sticks, stones, or mud. Rich and powerful people build bigger homes using expensive materials such as cut stone, timber, and steel.

People have lived in these cave homes in Turkey for thousands of years.

This book looks at homes from the earliest days to the present. It cannot include all kinds of houses, of course, but focuses on the different kinds of shelters people use. Houses vary from place to place, but whether we are rich, poor, or in-between, we need homes for shelter and protection.

This house in Iceland is an example of a very modern home.

Timelines

The information in this book is on a timeline. A timeline shows you events from history in the order they happened. The big timeline in the middle of each page gives you details of a certain time in history (see below).

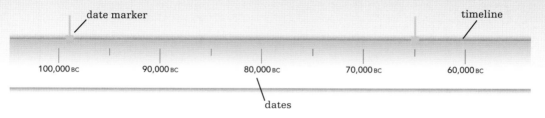

date marker

timeline

| 100,000 BC | 90,000 BC | 80,000 BC | 70,000 BC | 60,000 BC |

dates

The dates are not exact because early people did not keep written records. Other dates cover decades or centuries because they show what happened over a general period of time rather than on a precise date. The smaller timeline at the bottom of each page shows you how the page you are reading fits into history as a whole. You will read about homes from all around the world. Each entry on the main timeline is in a different color. This color shows you which continent the information is about. The map below shows you how this color coding works. Pale green indicates events that took place on more than one continent or worldwide.

North America

Europe

Asia

Africa

South America

Australia and Oceania

Worldwide

Caves and Campsites

Early people found shelter in caves or beneath trees or overhanging rocks. Caves were warm in winter and cool in summer. By about 33,000 BCE, people in France began decorating their caves by drawing on the walls. Today, it is thought that over 40 million people throughout the world live in caves. Many have electricity and modern furniture.

c. 98,000 BCE–present
Caves have been used as homes for thousands of years.

c. 50,000–35,000 BCE
Overhanging cliffs or rocks served as shelters while people hunted for game or gathered wild fruit.

100,000 BCE   90,000 BCE   80,000 BCE   70,000 BCE   60,000 BCE

c. 33,000–13,000 BCE
Early people decorated their caves with paintings, such as this one at Lascaux, France.

c. 18,000–13,000 BCE
HUNTING FOR HOMES

Many early people were **nomads**. They wandered from place to place hunting animals or gathering plants and roots to eat. They slept in tents or simple shelters that were easy to put up and take down when they wanted to move. The builders of this home in northern Europe used **mammoth** bones as a frame. They covered the bones with skins.

50,000 BCE   40,000 BCE   30,000 BCE   20,000 BCE   10,000 BCE

c. 13,000 BCE–present

Round huts, made of mud, stones, or clay, with straw roofs, have just one room. They are still used today in many places in the world.

Using What's Available

Around 9000 BCE, people began growing crops for food. They settled in one place and built permanent, or lasting, homes. They used whatever building materials were available.

c. 8000 BCE

In Jericho, an ancient city in the **Middle East**, houses were made of stone. Earlier houses were made of mud bricks that softened and collapsed when it rained.

| 8500 BCE | 8000 BCE | 7500 BCE | 7000 BCE | 6500 BCE | 6000 BCE |

c. 7000 BCE   TWIGS AND MUD

Many ancient people in western Asia, central Europe, and North America used **wattle and daub**. Corner posts held up a **thatched** roof of straw or **reeds**. Wattle is a pattern of crossed sticks or twigs. Daub is a mixture of water, mud, straw, and dung (animal waste) used to cover the wattle. The dung holds the mud and straw together so that the mixture lasts.

c. 3500 BCE
French borries were homes made of thin pieces of rock carefully piled on top of one another.

c. 3000 BCE
Egyptian farmers built homes of sun-dried mud bricks and thatched roofs. People slept on the roofs in summer.

5500 BCE	5000 BCE	4500 BCE	4000 BCE	3500 BCE	3000 BCE

c. 3200 BCE
Greek builders used **volcanic** stone covered with **plaster** to build homes that fitted snugly into cliffs overlooking the sea.

Renewable Materials

Early builders made bricks from mud, clay, and straw. They also used **reeds** and grasses. These materials are **renewable**; they replace themselves naturally. If a house needed repairs, fixing it was as easy as stepping outside and gathering more mud, reeds, or straw.

c. 3000 BCE–present

Inuit people in Alaska, Canada, and Russia made iglus (also spelled igloos) from blocks of snow. Iglus are strong structures that protect against cold weather outside while the inside is warmed by people's body heat.

3000 BCE	2750 BCE	2500 BCE	2250 BCE	2000 BCE	1750 BCE	1500 BCE

c. 3000 BCE–present

In Peru's lakes and swampy areas, people used reeds to build shelters. The houses are on islands made of woven reeds, which people continue to rebuild today.

c. 200 BCE–present YURTS

A yurt is a circular tent built on a frame and covered with felt or animal fur. **Nomads** in Russia, China, and Mongolia lived in yurts. When they moved on, they took the yurt with them. Today, yurts are popular vacation homes in North America, Europe, and in Japan and Korea. Modern yurts have electricity and toilets.

1250 BCE	1000 BCE	750 BCE	500 BCE	250 BCE	1 BCE

c. 500 BCE–present
Wattle and daub houses like this **replica** in County Wexford, Ireland, were common throughout Europe.

c. 100 BCE–present
Bamboo is light, tough, and long lasting. People throughout Asia use it for walls, roofs, floors, and furniture.

11

Homes to Show Off

As cities and villages grew, wealthy people built fancy homes to prove that they were important and powerful. Greeks and Romans used large blocks of cut stone, such as **marble**, for walls, steps, and even roofs. They also built tall columns, or posts, of polished marble.

c. 600–80 BCE PRIVACY

Homes of wealthy Greek and Roman families often had an atrium, or central room with an open roof, surrounded by columns. A pool in the center caught rainwater. Although they liked privacy at home, Greeks and Romans took baths with friends. Men and women went to separate public bathhouses to bathe.

600 BCE	500 BCE	400 BCE	300 BCE	200 BCE	100 BCE	1 BCE

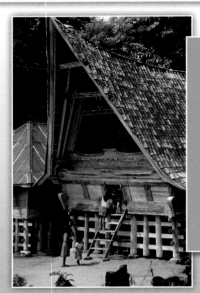

200 CE–present

The Toba Batak people of Indonesia built high-roofed houses on **stilts** to avoid getting flooded and to be safe from wild animals.

500 CE–present

The city of Sana'a in Yemen became a major center in Arabia and, over time, over 6,000 tower houses were built. Parts of these still exist now. They can be up to nine stories high and have a flat roof and painted walls.

100 CE   200 CE   300 CE   400 CE   500 CE   600 CE

400s CE

Rulers of the Ethiopian kingdom of Axum built a castle with stone walls and four corner towers.

600s CE

In Mexico, Mayan leaders lived in palaces made of cut stone.

Building for Protection

Castles were built like forts. The owner and his family lived in a strong stone home called a keep. Some castles included hidden rooms and secret passageways that led from beneath the castle out into the countryside. High stone walls, a water-filled trench called a moat, and a drawbridge protected the castle from attack. The moat stank. Castle toilets emptied directly into it.

1200–1300

Syrian rulers built castles in lonely mountain areas to protect against attack. Underground tunnels allowed those inside to escape.

900 CE	950	1000	1050	1100	1150	1200

900s–1500s CE

Stone towers and a moat protected this English castle from attack.

1200–1300 PUEBLO

The Anasazi people, who lived in the southwestern part of North America, made homes in rock cliffs by adding rooms on to existing caves. This dwelling at Mesa Verde, called the Cliff Palace, had 150 rooms. The location protected it from invaders.

1250   1300   1350   1400   1450   1500

1500s

Matsumoto Castle in Japan was a home for the local lord and his family as well as a fort. It is built on a stone foundation and has three moats.

Dark Days and Nights

During the Middle Ages (500–1500 CE) most houses were dark inside. Windows were small because glass was expensive and the stone walls could not support large openings without collapsing. Heavy curtains or **shutters** kept the cold out. They kept the light out, too. The only lighting came from the fireplace or candles.

1485–present   TUDOR HOUSES

Tudor houses in England had wooden frames set on stone foundations. The walls were made of **wattle and daub**. The roofs were made of **thatch**. Some houses today copy the Tudor style.

1480   1490   1500   1510   1520   1530   1540

1500s

In Turkey, many houses had two separate areas—one for family members and one for guests. The family area was called the harem.

1500s

Inca homes in Peru were made of stone and covered with mud or clay. There were no windows.

1600s–early 1900s

A tipi (or tepee) is made of wooden poles covered with animal skins. They can be taken down and moved when necessary. The Blackfeet, Crow, Lakota, and other Native American tribes used tipis.

1550   1560   1570   1580   1590   1600

1500s

Spanish people used paper or the greased skin of a sheep or goat to let light in and keep cold out during the winter. Iron bars on the windows protected the houses from break-ins.

Houses for Rich and Poor

Rich people lived in palaces and plantations with fancy furniture, while poor people slept on mats in simple huts. If they were lucky, poor families owned a table and one chair for the father. This is where we get the word *chairman* from.

1600s

The Shona people of Zimbabwe lived in small circular huts made of clay. As children grew, they were given smaller huts of their own nearby.

1669–1790

The French king's palace of Versailles, outside Paris, included a hall with 357 expensive mirrors.

1200 | 1250 | 1300 | 1350 | 1400 | 1450 | 1500

1200s–1600 COLD AND SMELLY HOUSES

In Europe's palaces and mansions, fireplaces provided the only heat. They sent smoke and soot through the rooms. People rarely bathed, so there were no bathrooms. Most Europeans believed dirt protected their body from illness. Smoky fireplaces and stinky people made for grimy, smelly neighborhoods.

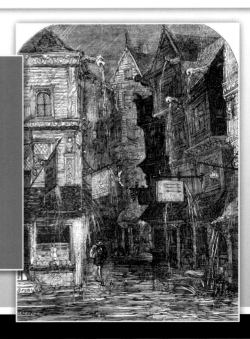

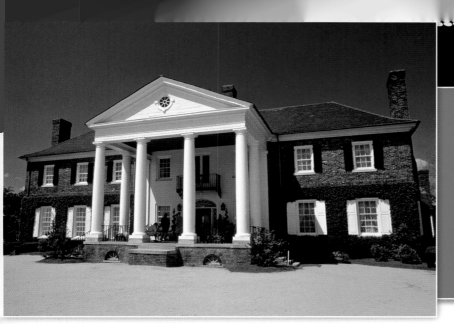

1600s–1800s

A cotton plantation called Boone Hall was built in 1681 near Charleston, South Carolina. The slave-owner's family lived in luxury in the main house.

| 1550 | 1600 | 1650 | 1700 | 1750 | 1800 |

1600s–1800s

Slaves who worked on plantations did not live in the main house. They lived in small brick houses like these on the plantation grounds.

Housing Millions

In the mid-1700s, Great Britain's **Industrial Revolution** brought workers to cities for factory jobs. As cities grew, housing became a serious problem. It remains so today. Half of the world's people live in cities.

1770s
People began to put flush toilets in their homes.

1862
In the United States, people could get land for free as long as they farmed it. The land was called a homestead. Homesteaders often started out living in simple huts made of **turf** or in wooden shacks.

1770   1785   1800   1815   1830   1845

1800s–present
Thousands of **immigrants** arrived in the United States needing housing. Blocks of apartments called **tenements**, like this one in New York City, quickly became overcrowded and run-down.

1897

Poor people in Brazil started to live in **slums** called *favelas*. Today, about 150,000 to 200,000 people live in a slum called Rocinha.

1920s

In Melbourne, Australia, large homes in the city became boardinghouses where many families lived together in crowded conditions.

1860	1875	1890	1905	1920		

1912–present SLUMS

A slum was set up in Kenya, where people made houses of tin and **wattle and daub**. Over one million people now live here without electricity, enough water, or **sanitation**. Throughout Kenya, over 2.5 million people live in slum housing. Almost every major city in the world has slum areas.

Suburbs

In the 1950s, middle-class people in Europe and the United States moved to **suburbs**, neighborhoods outside cities. They **commuted**, or took cars and trains to work. Today, suburbs surround most of the world's major cities.

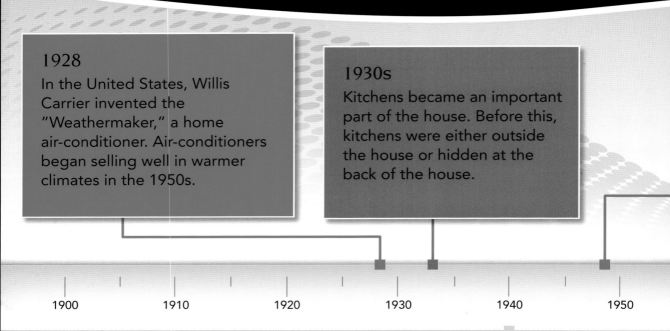

1928

In the United States, Willis Carrier invented the "Weathermaker," a home air-conditioner. Air-conditioners began selling well in warmer climates in the 1950s.

1930s

Kitchens became an important part of the house. Before this, kitchens were either outside the house or hidden at the back of the house.

1900   1910   1920   1930   1940   1950

1940s–present   COMFORTABLE HOMES

By the end of World War II in 1945, people wanted comfortable houses with labor-saving appliances. Boilers provided heat. Air-conditioning kept houses cool. Electricity powered lights, televisions, and kitchen appliances. Natural light flowed through big windows. These houses had bathrooms with flush toilets, baths, and showers. Houses were clean and sweet-smelling. People continue to expect these comforts today.

1948

Mobile homes began as camping trailers in the United States. By 1948 many were used as permanent homes. They were up to 9 meters (30 feet) long and included bathrooms. Today's mobile homes are even larger.

1950s–present

Homes in suburbs, like this one in Brazil, often look very similar.

1960   1970   1980   1990   2000

2000–present

Some suburbs include high-rise apartment blocks like these in Hong Kong's Happy Valley.

One of a Kind

Houses in the **suburbs** often looked alike. But some people wanted houses that were one of-a kind. **Architects** were happy to take on the challenge by creating brand-new styles.

1956

The design of this house in Caracas, Venezuela, includes strong steel beams to prevent it from falling down the hillside.

| 1950 | 1955 | 1960 | 1965 | 1970 | 1975 | 1980 |

1950s GLASS HOUSES

In Great Britain, Alastair Pilkington invented a new way of making large sheets of flat glass. This made picture windows, skylights, and glass walls possible. Several architects designed houses like this one, built in London, England, in the 1970s, that used large glass sheets. Glass houses seem to disappear into the background. They provide shelter, but not much privacy.

2003

This house in Auroville, India, has been built using materials from the past—cloth, mud-baked bricks, and **reed** mats —to create a new style.

1985   1990   1995   2000   2005   2010

1970s

Many people started restoring older houses. Poor areas of cities began to be **gentrified**.

1990s

People in the United States began to build huge houses on small plots of land. Often there were more bathrooms than bedrooms.

Houses of the Future

Maybe one day we will build homes in outer space or beneath the sea. In the future, builders may return to using materials from the past—**reeds**, mud, and the earth itself—in new and exciting ways.

1990s–present SUSTAINABLE HOUSES

Sustainable or "green" houses use **renewable materials** that can be recycled, and they use less energy than other houses. This eco-house in New Mexico is made of tin cans and mud. A wind turbine on the roof and solar panels provide energy. People will build more sustainable houses, or even eco-pods, in the future.

1990   1995   2000

Present

This "air tree" in Madrid, Spain, has plants on the inside and solar panels at the top. It provides enough energy to supply electricity to the apartments in the complex.

Present

This underground house in Wales, in the United Kingdom, uses earth for its roof and walls. Large glass windows provide light and a view of the sea.

2005   2010   Future

Future

Both the United States and China may set up bases on the moon. Houses on the moon will have to protect settlers from temperatures of −233 °Celsius (−387 °Fahrenheit) at night, to 123 °Celsius (253 °Fahrenheit) during the day.

Key Dates

98,000 BCE–present
Caves are used as homes.

13,000 BCE–present
Africans construct one-room huts of mud or clay with straw roofs.

7000 BCE–present
Wattle and daub is used in central Europe, western Asia, and North America.

3000 BCE
People in Peru use **reeds** to build shelters.

200 BCE–present
Nomads in Mongolia, Russia, and China live in yurts.

100 BCE–present
Asians use bamboo for walls, roofs, floors, and furniture.

900s–1500s CE
Castles throughout Europe have stone buildings, towers, and moats to protect their owners.

1200–1300
Syrian rulers build castles in remote mountain areas to protect against attack.

1200–1300
The Anasazi of southwestern North America make homes in rock cliffs by adding rooms onto existing caves.

1485–present
Tudor houses in England are built using wooden frames set on a stone foundation.

1500s
Spanish people use paper or the greased skin of a sheep or goat to let light in and keep cold out during the winter.

1600s–early 1900s
The Blackfeet, Crow, Lakota, and other Native American tribes live in tipis made of wooden poles covered with animal skins.

1770s
People begin to put flush toilets in their homes.

1800s–present
Thousands of **immigrants** in the United States live in **tenements**.

1880s–present
Slums called *favelas* become places where poor people in Brazil live.

1912–present
Africa's largest slum, in Nairobi, Kenya, is home to over one million people.

1950s
People begin to move to **suburbs** and **commute** to work in cities.

1970s
A process is invented to make large sheets of flat glass for picture windows, skylights, and glass houses.

1970s–present
People start to preserve and restore old homes.

1990s–present
Sustainable houses use less energy. Solar panels or wind turbines create energy to run houses.

Glossary

architect person who designs buildings

commute travel regularly over some distance. People who live in suburbs commute into cities to work.

gentrify change a house or area that is poor or run-down so that it looks nicer

immigrant person who comes to live permanently in a foreign country

Industrial Revolution time of rapid growth of factories that began in England in the mid-1700s and spread to many other countries

mammoth large, elephant-like mammal that used to roam the Earth

marble type of stone used for building that can be polished and comes in a variety of colors

Middle East region that includes southwest Asia and northeast Africa

nomad someone who moves from place to place

plaster thin paste spread on walls

reed straight stalk of grass

renewable material material that comes from a source that will not run out

replica exact copy

sanitation disposal of sewage and human waste

shutter movable cover for a window. Shutters are often made of wood.

slum thickly populated, run-down part of a city, where poor people live

stilt post supporting a structure built above the surface of land or water

suburb community built outside the city

sustainable saves energy and uses renewable materials. Sustainable houses may use energy from the sun.

tenement run-down and often overcrowded apartments

thatch material such as straw, rushes, or leaves used to cover roofs

turf surface of the ground covered with grass. Turf houses are built in places where there are no trees that can be used for building material

volcanic material left after a volcano erupts

wattle and daub building material of interwoven twigs plastered with mud or clay

Find Out More

Books

Barber, Nicola. *Homes Around the World: City Homes*. New York: Crabtree, 2008.

Gallagher, Debbie. *Homes Around the World: Mud, Grass, and Ice Homes*. North Mankato, Minn.: Smart Apple Media, 2008.

Manatt, Kathleen G. *Cool Science Careers: Architects*. Ann Arbor, Mich.: Cherry Lake, 2008.

McLeish, Ewan. *Sustainable Futures: Sustainable Homes*. North Mankato, Minn.: Smart Apple Media, 2007.

Shuter, Jane. *Picture the Past: Life in a Medieval Castle.* Chicago: Heinemann Library, 2005.

Websites

Learn about architecture at this website made just for kids.
www.archkidecture.org

This website will help you learn the history behind your own home.
http://americanhistory.si.edu/house/pdfs/webhouseguide.pdf

Learn what life was like in a colonial house by exploring this website.
www.pbs.org/wnet/colonialhouse/history/index.html

Index